Manual

Selected Writings 6

RICHARD BERENGARTEN was born in London in 1943, into a family of musicians. He has lived in Italy, Greece, the USA and former Yugoslavia. His perspectives as a poet combine English, French, Mediterranean, Jewish, Slavic, American and Oriental influences.

Under the name RICHARD BURNS, he has published more than 25 books. In the 1970s, he founded and ran the international Cambridge Poetry Festival. In the UK he has received the Eric Gregory Award, the Wingate-Jewish Quarterly Award for Poetry, the Keats Poetry Prize, and the Yeats Club Prize. In Serbia, he has received the international Morava Charter Poetry Prize and the Great Lesson Award, and in Macedonia, the Manada Prize. He has been Writer-in-Residence at the international Eliot-Dante Colloquium in Florence, Arts Council Writer-in-Residence at the Victoria Centre in Gravesend, Royal Literary Fund Fellow at Newnham College, Cambridge, and a Royal Literary Fund Project Fellow. He has been Visiting Associate Professor at the University of Notre Dame and British Council Lecturer in Belgrade, first at the Centre for Foreign Languages and then at the Philological Faculty. He is a Fellow of the English Association, a Bye-Fellow at Downing College, Cambridge, and Praeceptor at Corpus Christi College, Cambridge. His poems have been translated into more than 90 languages.

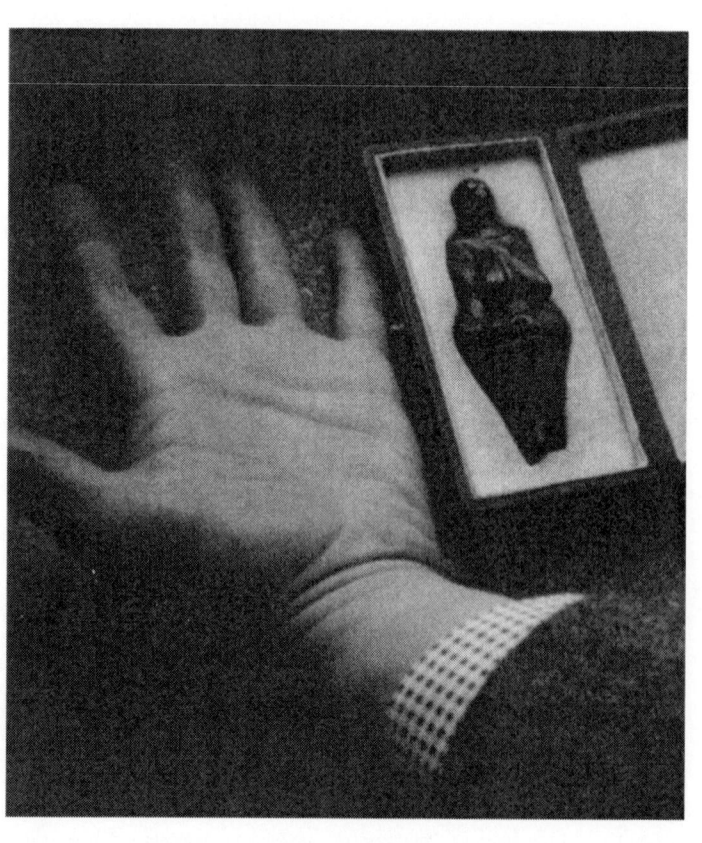

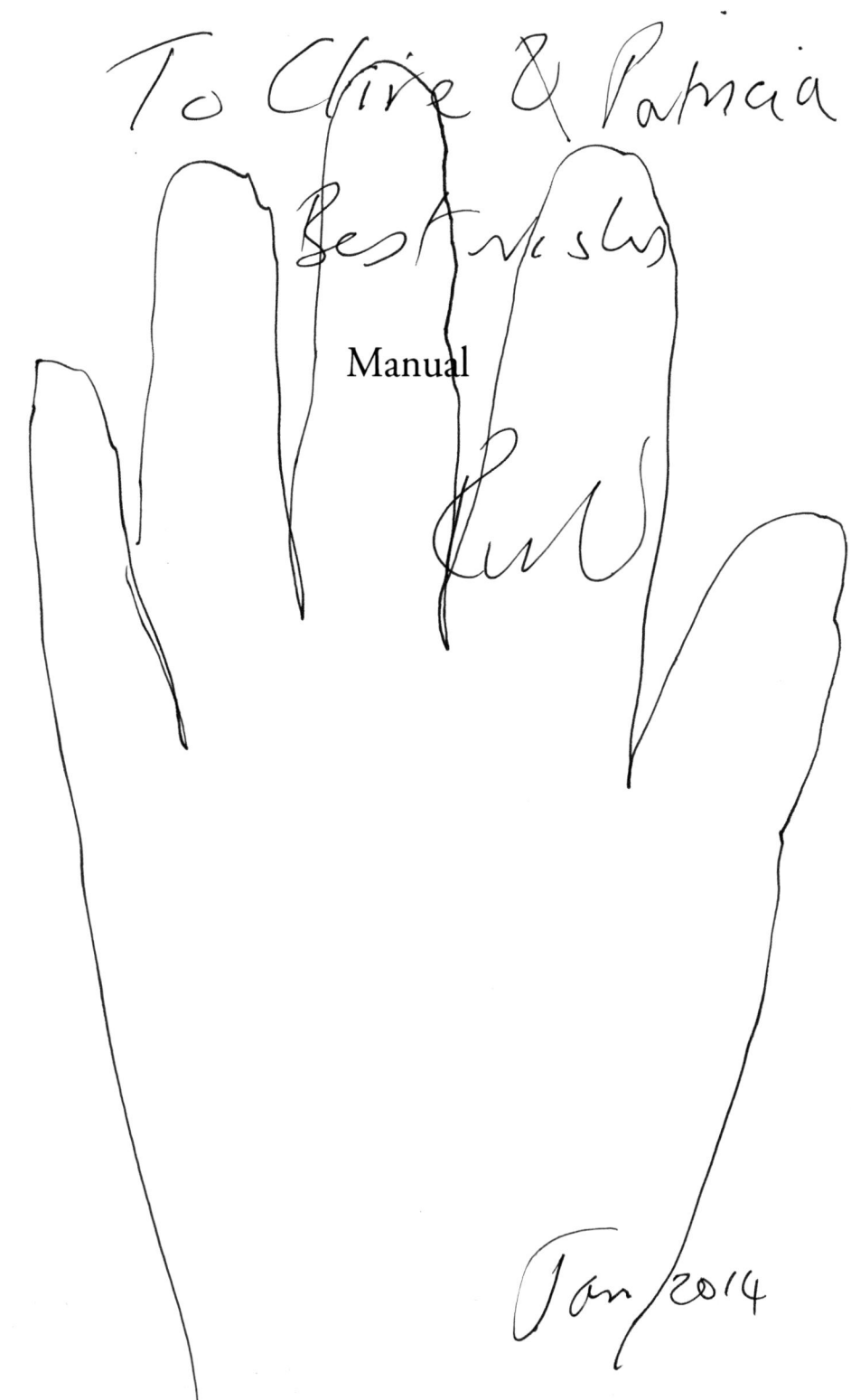

Manual

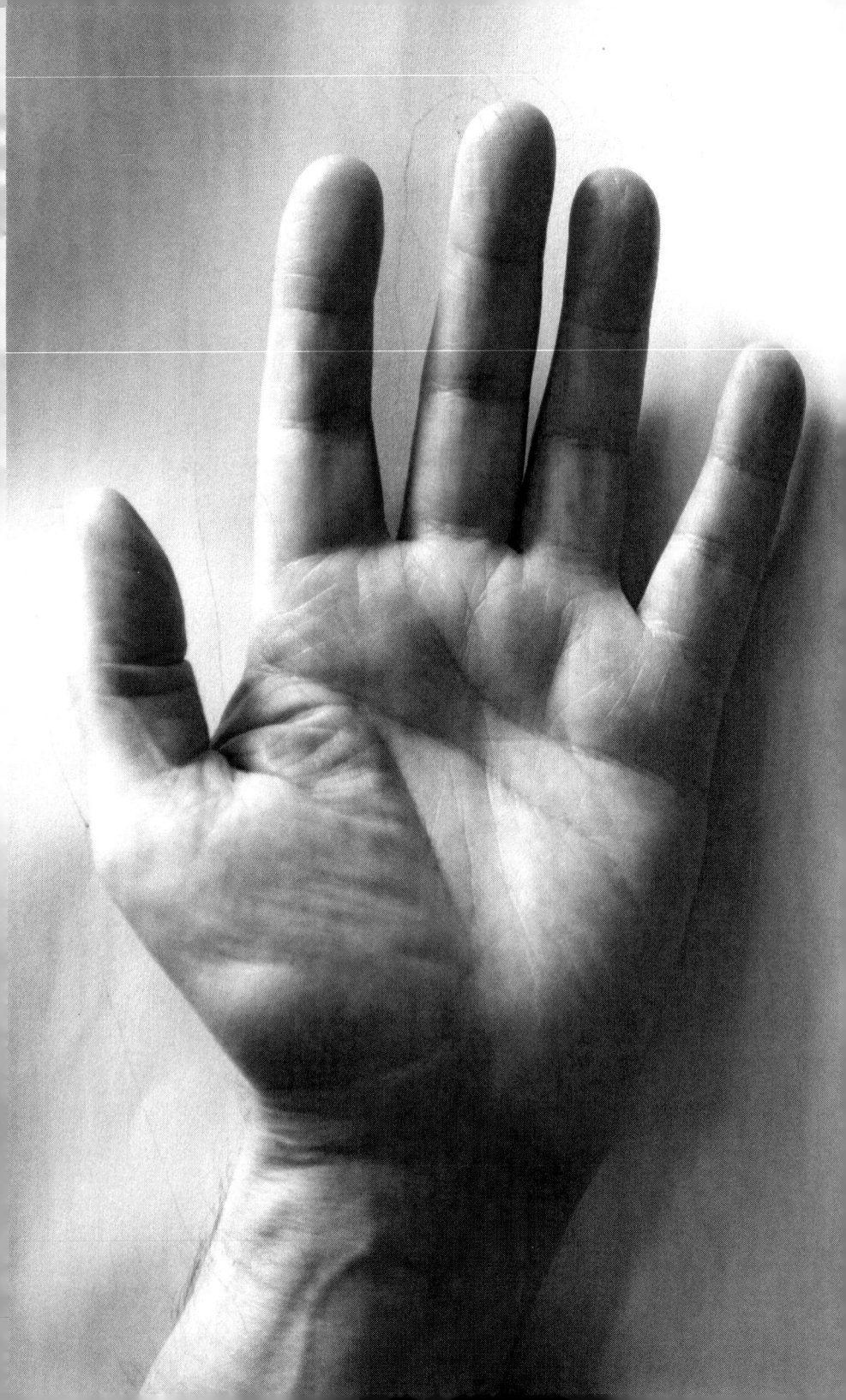

Manual

the first hundred

RICHARD BERENGARTEN

Shearsman Books

This edition published in the United Kingdom in 2014
by Shearsman Books Ltd
50 Westons Hill Drive
Emersons Green
BRISTOL
BS16 7DF

Shearsman Books Ltd Registered Office
30–31 St. James Place, Mangotsfield, Bristol BS16 9JB
(this address not for correspondence)

www.shearsman.com

ISBN 978-1-84861-325-6

Copyright © Richard Berengarten, 2014
Cover design © Will Hill, 2014
Cover and end-piece photographs © George Hill, 2014
All rights reserved

The right of Richard Berengarten to be identified as the
author of this work has been asserted by him in accordance
with Section 77 of the Copyright, Designs and Patents Act 1988.

Contents

Editorial Note
Acknowledgements

FRAME-PIECE I
Once mind taught hands, but these hands lead   3

MANUAL   *first twenty*
1. Here is a girl with her fists in her eyes   7
2. These hands touch things that are not things at all   7
3. Notice the statue's hands   8
4. These numb and empty hands hanging beside me   8
5. These skilled hands   9
6. Despite warnings from the other side of evening   9
7. But these hands cannot bring back the dead   10
8. Through these articulate wrists   10
9. Though winds write normal waves   11
10. Behind the hidden face of everything   11
11. These hands vainly cupping and dipping surfaces   12
12. These hands braving life's titanic oceans   12
13. That all the lights go out when I go   13
14. Out of wood feathers straw corn clay wax stone   13
15. Respected fellows and allies of these hands   14
16. She holds a wand of ivory and bone   14
17. The door she stands in is a blaze of light   15
18. Hands of victims clambered   15
19. You shall go with her when she beckons you   16
20. This left hand of mine   16

HOLDING THE DARKNESS   *second twenty*

   1. The woman sees the hunter   21
   2. The sun took the boy by the throat   21
   3. The last fifty feet   22
   4. The man beat his chest   22
   5. To move upwards   23
   6. From the deep round drum   23
   7. He looked down at his hands   24
   8. The sound of the drum   24
   9. Outside their yellow tent   25
  10. And as I drum   25
  11. So there they fly again   26
  12. This creature or thing   26
  13. How many of them   27
  14. I loved a boy once, said the old woman   27
  15. Scrolled writings in his left hand   28
  16. Beetles land and settle on his garments   28
  17. When getting into his carriage   29
  18. The children clap hands   29
  19. While voices of our fates   30
  20. And my guide took me   30

HOLDING THE SEA   *third twenty*

   1. They swam naked in the sea   35
   2. The woman woke early   35
   3. Outside the café   36
   4. The young wives toil uphill   36
   5. By the well   37
   6. Though there appears a little leeway   37
   7. Now we shall bathe you in soothing water   38
   8. The sea's fists lunged at him   38
   9. Toothless ghosts passion left behind   39
  10. This voice without body left in the bay   39
  11. The best survivors in these flat lands   40
  12. Gannets   40
  13. On the sea barrier   41
  14. Hands wave   41
  15. Now that you are leaving   42

16.	She woke the dozy child	42
17.	The child began wailing in her arms	43
18.	We went down to the river and it was dry	43
19.	After Du Fu	44
20.	Give me your hand	44

Manual *fourth twenty*

1.	Paleolithic Venus	49
2.	Midwives	49
3.	Hands of seagulls	50
4.	A tree owns nothing	50
5.	The afternoon was hanging on a thread	51
6.	She worked out in her garden	51
7.	The day was distinctive	52
8.	In the blur between could and will	52
9.	Cox's Pippin	53
10.	Look at this wall	53
11.	Before you close your eyes	54
12.	Somebody dropped a silver coin	54
13.	In the primary school	55
14.	When she did a handstand	55
15.	The face I stretch towards	56
16.	The last of the world's dragons	56
17.	All you need to do	57
18.	Hands of babes and infants	57
19.	These hands foresee and foretell	58
20.	Not one single one of the shadows	58

The Loved Ones *fifth twenty*

1.	The loved ones linger on the other shore	63
2.	On the other side of the river	63
3.	We stand on opposite banks	64
4.	In this house you have been before	64
5.	On this side, birdsong	65
6.	The loved ones line up	65
7.	The loved ones wring their hands	66
8.	The loved ones pace in circles	66

9. In Monument Park   67
10. There goes my father   67
11. You come back sometimes too   68
12. Between this side and that   68
13. Before boarding, please remember   69
14. Your misting eyes make out   69
15. Among these, we shall find no peace.   70
16. Across the river they point   70
17. Out of control   71
18. And now they're taking to the boats   71
19. In this gap between two worlds   72
20. Your hands play this film backwards   72

FRAME-PIECE 2
Curious how suddenly   75

Notes   77
Previous Publications by Richard Berengarten   78

Editorial Note

Manual, the sixth volume in the ongoing series of Richard Berengarten's *Selected Writings*, is an ambitious work-in-progress, a single poem, whose central theme is human hands.

This present collation is divided into five sequences and subdivided into one hundred small poems, with two frame-pieces at the start and end. Numerological patterning, an articulated feature of much of Berengarten's writing, occurs in each poem's formal structure: ten lines, ten fingers; two stanzas, two hands.

Acknowledgements

I am especially grateful to Brian Turner, of the Earl of Seacliff Art Workshop in Paekakariki, New Zealand, who designed and published each of the first four sections of this book as chapbooks in the 'ESAW mini series' (no. 10, 2006; no. 19, 2007; no. 23, 2008; and no. 25, 2009). Thanks also to Michael O'Leary, Mark Pirie and (the late) Daphne Dorrell, for advice, to Arijana Mišić-Burns for suggesting the title 'Holding the Sea', and to Paul Scott Derrick, Melanie Rein, Anthony Rudolf, Nasos Vayenas and Clive Wilmer for valuable comments on near-final versions.

Thanks also to the publishers, editors and translators of the following, in which some of these poems appeared: *Cambridge Literary Review* (1/1, 2009); *Eddie's Own Aquarius* (Cahermee Publications, Ireland, December 2006); *The Jewish Quarterly* (Summer and Winter 2007); *Las manos y la luz*, bilingual English and Spanish edition, trs. Miguel Teruel and Paul S. Derrick (Aula de Poesía, vol. 24, University of Valencia, Valencia, 2008); *Long Poem Magazine* (10, 2013); *Poetry Wales* (44/4, 2009); and *Speaking English: Poems for John Lucas* (Five Leaves Poetry, Nottingham, 2007).

I should also like to acknowledge the following authors, whose texts have given me ideas and inspiration: Confucius for *The Analects*; Andrew Duncan for *Savage Survivals Amid Modern Suavity* (Shearsman Books, Exeter, 2006); Henri Focillon for 'In Praise of Hands' in *The Life of Forms in Art* (trs. Charles Becher Hogan and George Kubler, Zone Books, New York, 1989); Edmond Jabès for *A Share of Ink* (tr. Anthony Rudolf, Menard Press, London, 1979); Emma Lew for *Anything the Landlord Touches* (Shearsman Books, Exeter, 2006); Robert MacFarlane for *Mountains of the Mind* (Pantheon, London, 2003); E. Dale Saunders for *Mūdra, A Study of Symbolic Gestures in Japanese Buddhist Sculpture* (Bollingen, Princeton, 1985);

David Sudnow for *Ways of the Hand, A Rewritten Account* (MIT Press, Cambridge, Massachusetts, 2001); Nasos Vayenas for *The Poet and the Dancer* (Kedros, Athens, 1979); and !Kewietenta-//ken, for poems in *the stars say 'tsau'* (tr. from the /Xam language, Antije Krog, Kwela Books, Cape Town, 2006).

RB
Cambridge
December 2013

*In memory of
my mother
Rosalind Burns
(1911-1968)*

As for me, I interpret hands neither from the body nor from the mind. The mind rules over the hand; hand rules over mind. The gesture that makes nothing, the gesture with no tomorrow, provokes and defines only the state of consciousness. The creative gesture exercises a continuous influence over the inner life. The hand wrenches the sense of touch away from its merely receptive passivity and organizes it for experiment and action. It teaches man to conquer space, weight, density and quantity. Because it fashions a new world, it leaves its imprint everywhere upon it. It struggles with the very substance it metamorphoses and with the very form it transfigures.

Henri Focillon

From an upright posture I look down at my hands on the piano keyboard during play with a look that's hardly a look at all. But standing back, I find that I proceed through and in a terrain nexus, doing singings with my fingers, so to speak, a single voice at the tips of the fingers, going for each next note in sayings just now and just then, just this soft and just this hard, just here and just there, with definiteness of aim throughout, taking my fingers to places, so to speak, and being guided, so to speak. I sing with my fingers, so to speak, and only so to speak, for there's a new being, my body, and it is this being (here too so to speak) that sings.

David Sudnow

Frame-piece 1

Once mind taught hands, but these hands lead
and chiral choral song begins.
It's not eyes but his hands that read
these passing notes at super-speed
body-voice integrates and spins.

Melodies fly on fingers' wings –
sounds yet unheard and unexplored
his whole (so-to-speak) body sings –
What cool flights! What meanderings!
What stings on strings in every chord!

Manual

the first twenty

The hand that is nowhere, that is the true home.
The Secret of the Golden Flower

1

Here is a girl with her fists in her eyes and here
another with a thumb in her mouth and here yet another
with head sunk deep in the bowl of her hands
as if they had all been deafened in a catastrophe
stilled and frozen in stone

Their gleaming skins are pearly under the moon
their foreheads have been branded by starlight
or perhaps lashed by the tail of a comet
their tunics are slightly soiled and torn and
their hands will never pick up a comb again

2

These hands touch things that are not things at all
memories dreams absolutions victories reflections
these hands also repeatedly pick such things up
responsibilities disadvantages obligations loyalties
take them on take them up refuse to let them go

Regardless of disputation dismissal attack and
despite ageing and gnawings of doubt and pain
these hands are capable of latching and indeed clinging
on stubbornly to certain things that are not things at all
that nevertheless can seem more important than life

3

Notice the statue's hands   how caringly
he tucked and folded chisel into marble
to free those moulded fingers from the rock
that would have locked them   still and undiscovered
in solid dark   like prehistoric bones

had not his own hands risen and in patience
spoken to stone by touch and by their probing
subtle persuasion   coaxed those perfect fingers
out of their sheaths   and for surrounding stone
substituted charged air   and vision   and history

4

These numb and empty hands hanging beside me
have been arrested by providence
Time has told them their time is nearly up
they have been cuffed on either side
by death's invisible officers

They would like to thread a needle
but can't pick up anything
they can't even pluck a string
trembling at the edges of empty pockets
they fumble for non-existent keys

5

These skilled hands descend from hawk-eyed
flint-shapers spear-hurlers and master-archers
who possessed the most accurate and unfaltering aim
the manifold talents of these hands came down also from
the most gifted of cunning and calculating craftswomen

mat and basket weavers and bone-needle workers
spinners and embroiderers and tapestry makers
collectors and breeders of grasses and tenders of gardens
preparers of dishes and drinks for ceremonies
brewers of analgesics and soporifics

6

Despite warnings from the other side of evening
from the reverse aspect of whatever season this is
from backs of unpolished windows
from whatever shape has been left by rotten fruit
from spaces unformulated and unregistered by words

these hands keep turning and re-turning
pages in a single book with no back cover
keep shuffling and reshuffling this pack of
uncounted and uncountable perfections you
might name *miracles glories eyeblinks*

7

But these hands cannot bring back the dead
who might have had more time
who should not have gone when they did
whose voices keep clamouring
even though they're dumb

from the mirror the lake the sky
from the coin the city the rose
from the book the photo the portrait
from the other side of everything
let us back in   give us another chance

8

Through these articulate wrists are channelled whispers
from the cool remnant hum of the universe's beginnings
like very distant drums   like bats' wing-beats
eight carpals   five metacarpals   fourteen phalanges
eight ghosts   five tigers   lesser palaces

On these receptive palms   stars have coded their densities
and in subcutaneous tissue   pencilled cloudy destinies
on these fingers   orbiting planets have printed circuits
engraining tips with furrows and ridges   like tree-rings
like galaxies   spiralling   like uncurling fern fronds

9

Though winds write normal waves across
its whispering changing meniscus   I know a chill lake
of blue green water   insulated among mountains
that never bore reflections whether beneath a roof
of stars so crystalline that upturned human eyes

against it might rest nowhere or so stunning under sun
that liquid cobalt here seem saturated in emerald
and though its water's surface yield no sparkle
and though all light to strike it here be drowned
do not doubt these hands will plunge me in and swim

10

Behind the hidden face of everything
there is a coin that has no back no tail
crowned head that rolls nowhere
but into cloudiness and bleary haze
where stopped clocks dissolve too

and that is where without knowing quite
what they're doing or wanting   these hands
follow to measure zeroes and their differences
to count the cost   of insubstantial substance
of no-things more than nothings

11

These hands vainly cupping and dipping surfaces
taking shimmerings for shapes of things as they are
and shadows for forms and patterns of what was once
and glimmers and gleams for shards of things to come
confusing real depths and reflections

these panicky hands   like ducks' or gulls' feet
can't help letting water slip past drop by drop
and like leaves of willows bordering a summer river
like boys' paper boats bobbing on playtime ponds
these paddling hands will drown

12

These hands braving life's titanic oceans
constantly splashing and flailing around
kicking and punching to keep afloat
will go down wreathed in seaweed
under coilings and curlings of waves

Fingernails will go on growing a little
longer after these hands grow cold but you
untouchable stars still I want more of you
and while these hands perish   bitter
the consolation you too will not be extinguished

13

That all the lights go out with me when I go
I am ashamed I've entertained this wish
for have I not extended one small finger
of this my better hand   into the palm
of a sleeping child

and felt his fingers clasp
and clamp my own involuntarily
as if I were a knotted rope he'll climb
into tomorrows past me
and I his spring and beam to steady hope

14

Out of wood feathers straw corn clay wax stone
out of sinew horn reed twig shell stem hide
these hands have painted cavewalls modelled gods
hewn coracles shaped triremes engraved cylinders
thatched garments woven roofs plaited bridges

drained swamps stained parchments spanned ravines
lettered cuneiform hieroglyphic rune
revealed taxonomies in monastery gardens
crafted sextants compasses microscopes
launched satellites around planets' moons

15

Respected fellows and allies of these hands
have coolly signed death warrants then dined
inspected slaves in quarries mines foundries
designed gaols torture rooms extermination chambers
issued instructions to builders and surveyors

pulled first triggers on victims over ditches
personally slit throats and kicked the dying in
dialled for bulldozers to destroy evidence
played chess poured wine opened their flies washed
then emailed superiors for further instructions

16

She holds a wand of ivory and bone
torchlike in her left hand   and in her right
she folds a drape across the battered zone
between the sudden darkening of light
and you   or what might still remain of you

She found her way from nowhere to this room
you have stayed in   and been stayed in   for years
to raise you up and lead you to your doom
your left hand in her right   to calm the fears
you know you must pass well into   and through

17

The door she stands in is a blaze of light
that scrolls behind her in a quilt of shades
and dazzlings edged with stunning blindnesses
spotting your vision in a hazed confusion
and she a dark breach in the afternoon

a starkness   a dense slab of silhouette
blocking all elsewheres from your space called *here*
and ramifying into corridors
of memory and dream surrounding it
until   stooping   she takes your hand in hers

18

Hands of victims clambered over
heaps of dead and dying companions
to scratch and dig wordless scrabblings
into the concrete of the very ceilings
as they themselves froze contorted

Hands of heroes dug tunnels under electric
perimeter fences surrounding floodlit camps
and before the margin of the treeline tugged
fellows out free to get away at least some
distance a little distance through the snows

19

You shall go with her when she beckons you
choicelessly yielding to the naked glory
and power of beauty coupled in her presence
All elsewheres and indeed all othernesses
memories   reminiscences   aspirations

and even those most dearly cherished hopes
you might expect to flood and saturate
such indeterminate intermediate zones
shall not appear behind her or around her
following the challenge in her first appearance

20

This left hand of mine now packing this page with script
and this right hand steadying the same page's edge
together reach out to your hands that hold and turn
the same copy in another time entirely your own
or click or flick an icon to resurrect its appearance

which curiously means that exceedingly far
across time and space and despite our mortalities
you and I join hands through poetry in a kind
of peace and harmony that is unshakeable and this
is a bond and a pledge and a gift

Holding the Darkness

the second twenty

Poetry will make use of her voice in order to show herself to us. The poet will be swayed by her. He will no longer be surprised when this voice, confiding, takes on for him the form of a hand: he will stretch out his own hands to her.

Edmond Jabès

1

The woman sees the hunter approaching
She smiles and asks him to anoint her
to rub a little of the creature's fat into the nape
of her neck and also just above the collar bone
He smiles and rubs her and she clutches him tight

She clutches the hunter so tight   his hands
disintegrate and decompose as they touch her
his hands melt into her   and his whole body
all his skin and organs and blood   everything
except his bones and teeth and nails and hair

2

The sun took the boy by the throat
The sun put his hands on the boy and throttled him
and out of the sun climbed a man
down the sun's own red and purple threads
because it was evening

and when the man's feet touched the earth
the man pounded his chest with his fists
he clenched his hands into fists and beat his chest
and he stamped as if earth were a hollow drum
and he roared with a lion's roar

3.

The last fifty feet were nearly vertical.
Wind drummed the tautened skin of his cheeks.
It felt as though the mountain was toppling over him.
The lashes on his right eye froze together.
To separate them, he pulled the lids apart.

He had one snow axe but he needed two.
He called his friend roped twenty feet below
Do we go on? Reply: *Of course we do.*
Using his right hand fingers as an axe-head
he stabbed them at the snow to get a hold.

4

The man beat his chest with his hands
and called to the forests rivers and lakes
I am morning and you shall remember me
then he turned and called
to the seas mountains and clouds

I am a builder and you shall remember me
and he stooped and scooped a handful of earth
and he mixed earth with a little water
and so a mud-daubed house
began to grow between his bare hands

5

To move upwards at all his whole body
had to hang back from the perpendicular
at angles between thirty and fifty degrees.
Grappling, swaying, balancing in the wind,
they made it to the kitchen-table sized

platform at the summit, where they clung
as to a mast, gale-buffeted and drenched
in pouring sunrise now the clouds had thinned,
the whole glacier below swathed and billowing,
buttoned in meltwater lakes, like shields winking.

6

From the deep round drum I beat with my
bare hands issues the call of the fanged snake
He rears and sways his sinuous head
He hisses and spits with his flickering tongue
and as from fire is dictated his command

His skin is patterned in red and black diagonals
His unfathomable eyes are gold and green
The call of his drum takes over my hands
and as I pound and pound its membrane
I am an invaded and occupied land

7

He looked down at his hands. From jabbing them
into the ice slope, three of his right glove's
finger coverings had ripped and shredded.
He couldn't feel them at all from the wrists down.
Three fingertips, exposed to freezing air

had taken on a waxed translucent sheen,
yellow, like aged cheese. Again and again
he stabbed them into the snow like a blunt chisel,
till, whooping like children, in relief and joy
they sledded the last shallow slopes on rucksacks.

8

The sound of the drum I beat and beat with my
bare hands has opened a gate in my head and
called my soul to a cavern huger than the world
and here the borderless and disembodied dead
are pounding the ground on parade in massed battalions

the graveyarded and the burnt-on-pyres
the pyramidded and vaulted   the shot and ditched
the hanged   the gassed   the drowned   the bombed
those whose tongues were cut out while still living
whether hale and young or varicosed and tumoured

9

Outside their yellow tent, later that morning,
he sat on a stone and stared at his glazed
finger pads. He tapped them against a rock
and they clacked as pencils or drumsticks might
echo against a surface of hollow metal.

He took out his penknife and began whittling.
On the flat grey rock between his knees
the heap of skin-shavings grew. He cremated
these offerings to the mountain with a lighter.
They charred and crackled with the scent of flesh.

10

And as I drum and drum with my bare hands
on the stretched skin membrane the thundering
of the massed dead pursues me everywhere
from the cavern they are holed up in and I know
each one of them is trying to clutch and crawl

along the endless tunnel through the unopenable
gate back up into this world and the closest
any of them can come to that impermeable threshold
is in the hollow echo of my hands drumming
which reminds them of the pattering of rain

11

So there they fly again
there they come and go
faces at the winter window
pressing hands on the pane
in a battering of snow

Glass frosts with breathless breath
shudders   in soundless wail
thoughts fade   histories pale
back these have come through death
through me   in snow and hail

12

This creature or thing or whatever
that keeps crashing against the windows is not
the wind but a man coming back as a bird
You can hear him screeching out there
above the brushing of the snows

across the roofslates and the dry whish
of smoke and drip of meltwater
His claws that were toes clutch branches
beak that was a mouth scrapes ice
wings that were hands flipper air

13

How many of them   lost down there
beggars imagination   shames belief
Even so these hands have mustered
enough courage   and although clumsy
and liable to trembling and unpredictable

abandonment   even by their own strengths
these hands can sometimes
prise open destiny's coffins
crack open time like a nut
break open death like an egg

14

I loved a boy once, said the old woman
in the hospice. He was pure when he fell.
In his last letter he told me
he was keeping himself for me.
He comes back when I'm sleeping.

He places fingers over my eyelids
and his smile protects my back.
He has turned into a white owl
perched on the eaves. His hands
have changed into wings to take me away.

15

Scrolled writings in the left hand and the right
raised, with tips of thumb and forefinger touching,
and the other three upright and facing outwards,
spell the passage of the written word into speech.
Hence action. Moulded in solitude, power rests

in the hands transmitting between them and the eyes
what is best described as a calm unflickering smile
arising from the core of a being who has remembered
that fear, though understandable, is unnecessary
and kindness and compassion can overcome it.

16

Beetles land and settle on his garments.
They adorn his lapels and sleeves
in crimsons and metallic blues. They worm
into his pockets and rest uncrushed there.
They creep out when rested and fly away.

Above his head rotates a ring of gnats
whirring anti-clockwise in silver rings.
Snails track liveried homes across his boots
and when he wakes he picks them slowly off
and puts them under leaves on shaded soil.

17

When getting into his carriage, he held its
mounting cord in his left hand and with his
right hoisted himself onto the platform. He
neither crouched nor stretched but moved
like a branch lifted on light wind.

He did not glance behind or raise his voice
irritably to man or animal. He spoke evenly
and went forward at a steady pace. He never
pointed or gestured with his hands but
rested them where everyone could see them.

18

The children clap hands
the echoes are deafening
even this side of the river
even though I can't see them
there's no mistaking what's going on

Though there's no ferry
and it's too deep for fording
if I can find a boat
I'll row over and if not I'll
swim across and join them

19

While voices of our fates
cackle like flames in wood
hands of fire tear
at every twig
crunch everything up

So may you be delivered
from hands of water
and hands of ice
and be consumed
by hands of fire

20

And my guide took me by the hand and led me
into a darkness that was not a darkness and
into a silence that was not a silence and paused
and said in a voice as quiet as running water
You have come from a country where poetry

is so trammelled up in clever elegance
that only opacity is praised and prized
but if you will listen and open up your hands
I shall teach you a poetry transparent and pure
as the wind and as impossible to pin down as light

Holding the Sea

the third twenty

Poetry is a criticism of life.
       Matthew Arnold

Poetry is a criticism of death.
       RB

1

They swam naked in the sea
and sea-water dripped from their skin
and they stroked and licked each other
in the shallows, both of them
drenched in sea

Later   with wavelets lapping them
they pooled sea water
in cupped hands
and for an instant saw the moon
reflected in each other's palms

2

The woman woke early   kneaded and shaped the dough
sprinkled poppy seeds all along its length
basted it with a fine brushing of oil   and baked it
and when her man and children came out
she cut the loaf with her hands to feed them

She cut the loaf with her hands sharp as razors
strong as oaks   more supple than the sea
and with her touch as tender as rain on sand
she fed her man and children out of the depths
of the mineral earth with her baked ground seeds

3

Outside the café underneath the plane tree
the old sailors play backgammon
Little they know or care about pasts or futures
who once chugged out past overhanging islands
and caught shoalfuls of fish in their long nets

Islands reached stony fingers out to grab them
Hidden rocks and reefs sharpened their nails
Waves grew claws to slash at them and snatch them
Darkness itself unleashed invisible talons
and now they sit outside the café like ordinary men

4

The young wives toil uphill ferrying water
and by the well the old ones knit and sew
They are reeling in the ships far out at sea
darning and mending aftermaths of wrecks
snipping and bordering frayed hems of lives

Even the strengths and directions of winds
and patterns of eruptions on ocean floors
get stitched by their gnarled fingers
and what they do   they do
scarcely noticing the effects they achieve

5

By the well the *tricoteuses*
can afford to chat and pause
Their hands are in no hurry
Once they had dancers' feet
Now they are all fingers

As they chatter about this and that
delicately intent but
seemingly without effort
their hands carry on regardless
like busy spiders

6

Though there appears a little leeway for movement
there isn't much really   and even though we feel
free to pour apparently limitless air past and between
fingers   these can barely stroke the counterpane
let alone your face   let alone pray

Officious death is waiting to peel fingerprint from flesh
flesh from subcutaneous tissue and so on down
to bare bones and then all the delicate sensations
you and I have shared and given each other
will rattle like pebbles shackled under the tide

7

Now we shall bathe you in soothing water
misted in eucalyptus and honey-spirals
and water's own hands will glove you
soul in body   body in soul
until they are coterminous

So rest your head a little before the end
of your flesh-trek   blood-voyage   bone-trip
and the gnawing of everything by nothing
till all that's left of your softnesses is nothing
and your skull is a puckered seashell.

8

The sea's fists lunged at him, collared him
and held him in a loose, careless embrace
until he numbed and swelled. Then the sea's
thorough fingers, examining and probing,
pulled him down into her primeval world.

As if with elegant fins and sails, he flew
among coral chambers and corridors
of rock, ascending and descending each
of their levels and spirals, until the sea's fingers
brushed and rolled him back on her briny beach.

9

Toothless ghosts passion left behind
have no need of hands
What is there to caress
or touch in the other
world but dreams of dreams

Some they say succeed in going
even farther than that land without borders
I don't quite believe it
I can't imagine being
without desire

10

This voice without body left in the bay
by a dead man now belongs to the water
that batters and roars against
this striated brocade of rock and slate
polishing and repolishing it

Surely you couldn't be out looking
for *harmony*, forced as you are to lean
against this savage wind's counterweight
as it buffets you like a puppet
as if with invisible hands.

11

The best survivors in these flat lands were
long-armed   short-legged   barrel-chested
men and women who shifted boulders
from mud, drained lakes and put up walls
against sea and river borders with bare hands.

Waist-deep in uncrushable water
of insect-infected swamps, they stooped,
crouched, pressed and shoved to sink
poles as foundations so houses could rise
and marshes be turned into fields.

12 *Gannets*

There must be a dozen of them wheeling
and dipping over the bay, more than
a hundred feet up from the water and two
hundred from the cliff where we stand
and every now and then one of them peels

off and dives stupendously at rocket speed
plummeting into the water at a not quite
vertical angle and a moment or so
later surfaces with a fish in its mouth
and a blander-than-ever expression.

13

On the sea barrier below the golf course
outside Ballycastle we stood and looked out
at the Mull of Kintyre twenty five miles north east
muffled in summer haze
and one of us, I think it was you, said

People must have rowed or sailed countless times
across this sea between Scotland and Ireland. Think
of the commerce – migrations, marriages,
and how these mattered, and fishermen and sailors
who grasped oars and ropes in their hands.

14

Hands wave   The ship
is leaving   We may not
see each other again   old friend
this side of the grave
But when we're out of sight

these same hands   like eyes
thanks to other hands
will see across huge distances
and carry each other's
messages across the waves

15

Now that you are leaving,
your hands curled already over the oars
balancing them and twirling them
grooved in their oil-slicked locks,
take the boy with you.

Look back as you row out
and let your gaze pass through and over us
to the hills' flanks, gloried in morning.
With his hand on the tiller, the boy
will guide you out and on.

16

She woke the dozy child and lifted him
to snuggle into her shoulder,
his head lolling against her neck,
legs dangling each side of her left hip,
eyes closed fast and lips set in a smile

and that is how she carried him
down to the sea and on to the boat
where she cradled him across her knees,
covered, except for his face, in a small blanket
while the man rowed them out to one of the islands.

17

The child began wailing in her arms
and she straddled him across her lap,
widening the arch of her legs, supporting
his back along its whole length with
her left forearm, while with her right hand

she unslung her left shoulder drape
and, easing out her breast, touched its engorged
nipple. Turning the infant around, cradling him
now with her right arm, she put his mouth
in place and sighed as he began to suck.

18

We went down to the river and it was dry
so we walked across it. But the bank
on the other side was too steep. Wherever
we tried to get a foothold it crumbled
and we fell back into shale and dust.

We walked back to the other side and stared
at the cliff face and cursed. Now we've gathered
at the top of the shallow path and keep gazing
at the mountain. We're working on ways
of cracking an entry there.

19 *After Du Fu*

Drains haven't yet dragged me
into them. Sewers' sluices and stenches
haven't yet doused my fire. My heart
is still whole and my hopes soar high,
high enough, at least, to pen poems.

Twenty years ago seems a breath away.
Twenty years hence will be nearing or past
my end. For this reason my sure right hand
holds this book while my subtler left one
writes poems clear as crystal water.

20

Hey you   give me your hand
No   you won't fall
You're safe   and now
the other one   Easy now
Hold on tight   with both hands

Far shall we go and
high and nothing
will pull us apart
Clear skies and hills
overlooking the sea await us

Manual

the fourth twenty

In the area between is and was are leaves
                      Wallace Stevens

Donnons nous la main
                  Guillaume Apollinaire

1

Here is the paleolithic Venus of Lower Věstonice
in her padded box placed on the concrete windowsill
of the 4th floor office of the Director of the Museum
of Moravia   Brno   Czechoslovakia   March 1977
discovered July 1925   under a layer of ash

her left leg broken off   estimated
the oldest clay-fired ceramic in the world
moulded between 27,000 and 31,000 years ago
before Mnajdra   before Lepenski Vir   before Atlantis
and the living left hand next to her is mine

2

Midwives calling *Push* and *Breathe* and *Push Now*
who cradle mucus-stained bloodied heads of infants
falling bawling into this world are careful to guard
the delicate fontanelle for this is said to be a heavenly
gate surrounded by discernible rings of power and light

and because the first organ of a newborn child to emerge
into its birthplace is its glory   this the midwife
cradles between her gifted hands and releases just
before the following head and body are squeezed out
and she knots umbilicus and disposes of placenta

3

See hands of seagulls fan and part the air.
They wake and scream along the wake we make.
Heads turning, cushioned on apparent nothing,
they beat and fold the winds. At their command
invisible currents move and carry them.

Whatever we breathe they breathe. But this air –
fluted, fanned and streamlined, poured and swept
by hands of seagulls balancing on wind-gusts –
is to them *terra firma*, ground they dance on,
invisible hollow drum they stroke and beat.

4

A tree owns nothing
but basks in the singular
scarcely discernible
circle of glory linked
by branches through air.

Where do I belong? Why,
wherever you're planted
in forest or prairie or garden.
So spoke the wind to a girl
through fingers she peered between.

5

The afternoon was hanging on a thread
of silvered light and everything was perfect
at and inside that moment in an intense
brilliance. She took the key out of her bag
and opened her own door and went inside

and walked through her own house opening blinds
to let the curious light permeate in. She threw
open windows and the French windows
onto the garden where still the afternoon
hung on its silvered thread as she went out and through.

6

She worked out in her garden, pruning roses,
clearing bracken, plucking out roots of weeds
and creosoting the border fence between
her plot and her neighbour's. It made sense
too, to run the mower over the lawn.

She worked like that from midday until evening
taking small breaks for sandwiches and teas
as if with someone else, though there was no-one.
All day it was a golden afternoon.
Night followed, flowering a horned moon.

7

The day was distinctive, precious
and distinctly ordinary. It was autumn.
Everywhere you looked, a blaze of leaves
hung, flaked, quivered, wavered and floated
from trees along Watton Road and its front gardens.

Humming, she wheeled the buggy past
bungalows, her son slouched in it sleeping,
and daughter walking beside, holding
onto its handle. In the park she would give them
turns on mini-slide, seesaw and swing.

8

In the blur between *could* and *will*
on the edge between *might* and *shall*
on the border of *want* and *do*
things in the mind mingle with desire
and action calls the doer to perform.

To *happen* means unravelling into now
of latent and subliminal intents
packed larger in potential than enormities
of actual occurrence. Of that, destiny's
single hand slow clapping makes doubly sure.

9

You hold in your left hand the first Cox's
Pippin of September. It looks at you
as your fore and mid-fingers and thumb
rotate it, on one side streaks of red and
green, like wood grain, and on the other

striations of red in various depths and
intensities. Every part of its polished skin
reflects light. And its pips still rattle, as
they did in childhood. This apple an Eve
might have picked and handed to an Adam.

10

Look at this wall now   Here is a piggy
and here a dog with floppy ears
and here a man's face with a big nose
and here his mouth opening   very wide
and here a bear   and here a lion

and now they all have their mouths open
the pig the dog the man the bear and the lion
and if it were not for these hands holding things up
all these shadows would gobble one another up
and darkness completely cover over everything

11

Before you close your eyes now look
at what these hands are making on the wall.
Fluttering to each other now they've turned
into two green and purple humming birds,
their yellow pointy beaks almost touching.

And now they're joining up into a single
butterfly that's lighting up the face
of dark in masks and marks of brightness
laced in scintillating blues and silvers
with black and gold orbs on its scaly wings.

12

Somebody dropped a silver coin.
It span and rolled and tumbled
into a crevasse, where it melted.
From a volcano, a bubble popped
and in the upper air its filmy skin

congealed into a drop that froze
and landed. A boy out walking
picked it up and kept it in his pocket.
He clutched it whenever he needed
to think of an answer or make a real wish.

13

In the primary school workshop a nine year old
boy called Shane stood up and read the poem
he'd been making. As he stopped a hush swept
through the eighty or so children of his age
sitting on the wooden floor of the assembly hall

and in that silence we were held in an almost
palpable ring of astonishment and awe, made
by Shane's words rippling on and through air
into our ears, until one child put hands together
and started clapping and everyone joined in.

14

When she did a handstand, treading invisible air
she held the world up a little higher than usual
and clouds underneath her fled and the sun grinned
and when she waved, four hundred million people
on the other side of the world murmured in sleep

and stirred as a slight breeze lifted their spirits
and an epidemic of smiles instantly burst
and rippled down succeeding centuries
and simultaneously flooded back to nudge
the weightless dead into innumerable smiles.

15

The face I stretch towards dissolves before
my eyes can make her out, in mist and dark.
With hands prepared to see, I reach, therefore,
past all that intervenes, to find the mark.
Hands fill all space between us with their labour.

However minuscule the gap between,
however close, however intimate –
her face, though known too well, remains unseen,
and that space, never less than infinite,
means my search, knowing-by-touch, must last for ever.

16

The last of the world's dragons flaps his wings
then takes off in vast gusts. Leaping, he breathes
fireballs at grey cloudbanks and dissolves them.
As highest factor hidden in the laws
of what *once was* – now he tucks in his claws.

One last puff from his nostrils, and he soars.
The valley children gather down below,
faces right-angled upwards, mouths awed ovals,
A gap opens in time, a timeless pause.
They clap their hands in sorrow and applause.

17

All you need to do   said my three
and a half year old grandson in my dream
is take green playdough and pull
and twist it into a body and take blue
playdough and cut it into four strips

and take red playdough and roll it
into a lozenge for a head and put them
all together and there you've got a
brand new dragon   you blow into it
he said   and then it breathes out fire

18

Hands of babes and infants
carry you into the future
and you and you and you
farther than you could ever
recognize or imagine

Don't be afraid
you won't be forgotten
this spirit into your
hands I commend and
yours and yours and yours

19

These hands foresee and foretell
for the future that is now
for the future that is already
for the future so and such
for the future sown and sewn

These hands forespell and foretune
futures not yet seen or scene
futures never to be seemed or seamed
for was-it-not-always
for the unexpected

20

Not one single one of the shadows
will hurt or wrap you around
or swallow or bash or push you
nor so much as lay a single finger
on you or even graze you

so long as I'm here watching over you
you shall be looked after
in sleep and waking and
my hands shall be with you
here child for ever

The Loved Ones

the fifth twenty

It's painful and difficult, the living are not enough for me
first because they do not speak, and then
because I have to ask the dead
in order to go on farther
       GEORGE SEFERIS

1

The loved ones linger on the other shore
behind dreams or before them. There is
much sighing and weeping but no-one listens.
Hands that intervene give functional aid.
Black hands and white hands mingle together.

Their need is for *Sicherheit*, not food and water.
Not understanding, not compassion,
not charity. The old men of the villages
were beaten up by militias
who came in trucks and carried clubs and guns.

2.

On the other side of the river, in a three
storey house, a gabled double window
set in its sloped roof opens. A young girl's
face looks out. She sees me, smiles and waves.
She waves and waves. She cups her hands.

She calls. Standing on this side, I wave too,
smile back. Though I can't make out her face,
I know her. I know I know her. Somebody
once very close. But I can't be sure who. Or
which of us is alive. Or dead. Or unborn.

3

We stand on opposite banks
and wave at each other. We make out
each other's shapes. But our features
are blurred and our voices can't
be heard because of wind

and distance, unbridgeable.
As I watch, I hear my own voice
muttering, I'm alive, you're dead.
Then I remember, when you hear this
the dead one will be me. Not you.

4

In this house you have been before
many times   you know it as soon as
your fingers push open the garden gate
and you find yourself in a place that belongs
to memory   or memory of memory

and you walk from room to room
and a wind blows through   and through you
all windows being open   but there's no
scent of the sea that's been calling you
even though you can hear her voice

5

On this side, birdsong
blots out whatever sounds
come from those who belong
where time has stopped, and hands
and arms lie crumbled at the feet of statues.

'No bridge exists,' caw the crows
'to the other side, nor ever did.'
'Why, there was one once,' replies
a gold-beaked blackbird. 'Its broken
back lies buried under ravening waves.'

6

The loved ones line up. Queuing – or on parade?
They need more attention, more time, more
love. None of which you can any longer
spare them. Bread is not enough. Nor is devotion.
Nor is Hope, which is for them impossible.

In this world's light the loved ones insinuate
themselves into everything, everything into themselves.
They need to be mirrored everywhere.
Shading their eyes with their hands
they see only horizonless haze.

7

The loved ones wring their hands.
They can't actually see you.
Then they shade eyes with hands
and stare towards you. It's hard to make out
what these gestures of theirs mean.

Many times they strung and cast nets together.
Now they pull nothing out of the sea.
Their time for working and gossiping is over.
Instead they shuffle, gazing across the border,
or stand like statues. Like scattered trees.

8

The loved ones pace in circles,
then they stop and stare.
Who knows if they make out
anything but haze or cloud
or see right through you and me.

One of them points, waves and jumps
then cups his hands and shouts. But
there's too much gusting off the estuary
to make out words, and on this wind
sounds get blown further and further away.

9

In Monument Park, close by a broken bridge,
slouches a small boy. He cups his hands and calls.
I can almost hear. But can't make out his words.
He jumps and stamps. He buzzes back and forth
like a fly against glass. Then, suddenly, he freezes.

Through his trumpet of hands, my stilled boy calls,
cataleptic in marble, his mouth an oval zero.
Singly and in clusters, behind him, other statues
wake. They blink, yawn, stretch, stare around.
Waves break beneath them like eggshells.

10

There goes my father, tottering among the ruins,
a white stick in his hand and on his back a guitar.
I wonder if he still plays, skilled fingers fluttering
into honeyed melodies like blue-winged hummingbirds
or if his gnarled hands have forgotten how to sing.

And that crone beside him, with her sunken bony grin,
ragged hair, back bent, shrunk from remembered height,
in whose body I was grown, who nourished me with her blood,
from whom I fell unscathed, whose milk poured into me,
leading him by the arm, pointing into blank distance.

11

You come back sometimes too, although you
aren't supposed to, with eyes smiling
and welcoming hands. Yours open, stretch down,
as mine lift towards you – or vice-versa – and
together we sway in uncanny, unhesitant dance.

Betrayals, blames, shames and many contrived lies
textured our time together. Since we shan't meet
again in flesh, are these apparitions
reminders of garnered loss, or compensations
for wished-for states we carelessly tossed away?

12

Between this side and that
flows a river consisting
of utterly nothing
The ferryman who takes you
one way only is a figment

His sail-less boat is floated
across that total stillness
not by hands of humans
but beat of invisible wings
under your eyelids

13

Before boarding, remember,
even if in wish and dream, screens
between *here* and *there* have minuscule
cracks, folds and peepholes in them,
our frontier is not passable

both ways, nor are twin passports,
reciprocal visas or round trip tickets
available to anyone bound for our
country, departure gates to which
are indelibly marked *No Return*.

14

Your misting eyes make out
your way down green-slimed steps
into a creaking swaying boat,
oars ready in their locks.
From its ring in the jetty wall

you uncoil its mooring rope.
Outward you row, sea
breeze in your lungs, sea tang
in your nostrils, and in the back
of your head no onward vision.

15

Among these, we shall find no peace.
Better be burnt to nothing than long like them
to return. We carp neither at their honouring
when they flit among us, nor at probing them
for answers, which they'll never surrender.

They travel, trawl, travail with us. And keep
straining to touch. With clammy outstretched
fingers, they skim, perch, clutch. They beseech,
warn, prophesy. Shrinking, we listen.
Do our best to follow. Ask no questions.

16

Across the river they point, wave, jeer. They
cup hands, lift heads, screech, beat chests
with one hand and ululate, the other slapping
their mouths. I can't make out a word, this offshore
wind is so strong. But know they are taunting.

What could be worse than being cast for good
among them, belonging to them entirely –
even though soon I know winds will drop
and I shall be called too. I too shall hear
their summons to cross over.

17

Out of control, now the loved ones
have infiltrated chisels, files, pliers into
their cells, broken into staff-rooms, smashed
cabinets and computers, scattered documents,
stolen keys, clubs, mallets, jacks, steel clippers,

switched off currents to their entire island,
cut holes in barbed wire, and broken through
perimeter fences. Surviving guards cannot
be counted or counted upon. They have melted
like shadows into surrounding marshes.

18

And now they're taking to the boats,
pouring over this side in a slow unstoppable
stream. Some have outboard engines. Some sail,
some paddle, some row. Some dip and swish
hands to propel them through water.

Leaky barges, luggers, junks, clippers, yachts,
coracles, canoes, tubs – each beach along our shores
lies prone to their landings. Soon our whole coast,
cliff-threaded bays and hill-protected coves,
will be colonised. Conquered. Completely.

19

In this gap between two worlds
along their borders, into No Man's Land,
these hands toss pebbles
but there's no surface to bounce on.
Endlessly they fall.

No, that sound is not of plashing
stones plummeting into water
or protest of leaves against wind.
It is a thrum of wings
under your eyelids.

20

Your hands play this film backwards.
They plough time down to its marrow.
Seeds they sow now will be harvested yesterday
where, hungry and thirsty for news,
the loved ones stretch out hands.

Everything your hands do makes sense.
Now that you have finished making this,
under their mountains the loved ones
who have been listening and watching attentively
clap hands in unison.

Frame-piece 2

Curious how suddenly, Rosalind,
out of a buried remembering,
I find you in those gestures
I used to see you making, which
now, without my reckoning,

bloom again out of my own hands,
as though yours, tenacious roots,
had grown grains of your own
ways of doing and achieving things,
deviously, through and into mine.

Notes

Manual was first conceived in New York on Saturday, March 1979 (St. Patrick's Day). The collation published here was completed in Cambridge on Saturday, August 4, 2012. Its gradual unfolding and composition occurred in many places at many times.

When the book is closed, the hands on the covers are in the gesture of submission or prayer. When they are open, their gesture is of offering or receiving.

The frontispiece reproduces a grainy photo of the 'Venus of Dolní Věstonice', which I took in the office of the director of the Museum of Moravia, Brno, with his kind permission, in the late 1970s. This photo is the source of 'Paleolithic Venus' (p. 49).

Several sequences and poems are dedicated, as follows: 'Holding the Darkness', *the second twenty* (pp. 19–30) to Anthony Rudolf; 'Holding the Sea', *the third twenty* (pp. 33–44) to Norman Jope and Paul Scott Derrick; 'Outside the café' (p. 36) to Anastassis Vistonitis; 'On the sea barrier' (p. 41) to Melanie Rein; 'Hands wave' (p. 41) to the memory of Ian Jack; 'Manual 4', *the fourth twenty* (pp. 47–58) to Lara Burns and David, Oscar, Owen, Imogen and Alex Lightning; 'The last of the world's dragons' (p. 56) to Gully Burns; 'Manual 5', *the fifth twenty* (pp. 61–72) to Nasos Vayenas; and 'Among these, we shall find no peace' (p. 70) to Jim Fitzgerald.

RB
Cambridge
December 2013

Previous Publications by Richard Berengarten

The Selected Writings of Richard Berengarten
    Vol. 1 *For the Living: Selected Longer Poems, 1965–2000*
    Vol. 2 *The Manager*
    Vol. 3 *The Blue Butterfly* (Part 1, *The Balkan Trilogy*)
    Vol. 4 *In a Time of Drought* (Part 2, *The Balkan Trilogy*)
    Vol. 5 *Under Balkan Light* (Part 3, *The Balkan Trilogy*)

Poetry (written as Richard Burns)
    The Easter Rising 1967
    The Return of Lazarus
    Double Flute
    Avebury
    Inhabitable Space
    Angels
    Some Poems, Illuminated by Frances Richards
    Learning to Talk
    Tree
    Roots/Routes
    Black Light
    Croft Woods
    Against Perfection
    Book With No Back Cover
    Do vidjenja Danice (Goodbye Balkan Belle)

As Editor
    An Octave for Octavio Paz
    Ceri Richards: Drawings to Poems by Dylan Thomas
    Rivers of Life
    In Visible Ink: Selected Poems, Roberto Sanesi 1955–1979
    Homage to Mandelstam
    Out of Yugoslavia
    For Angus
    The Perfect Order: Selected Poems, Nasos Vayenas, 1974–2010

Prose
    Keys to Transformation: Ceri Richards and Dylan Thomas
    Imagems (1)

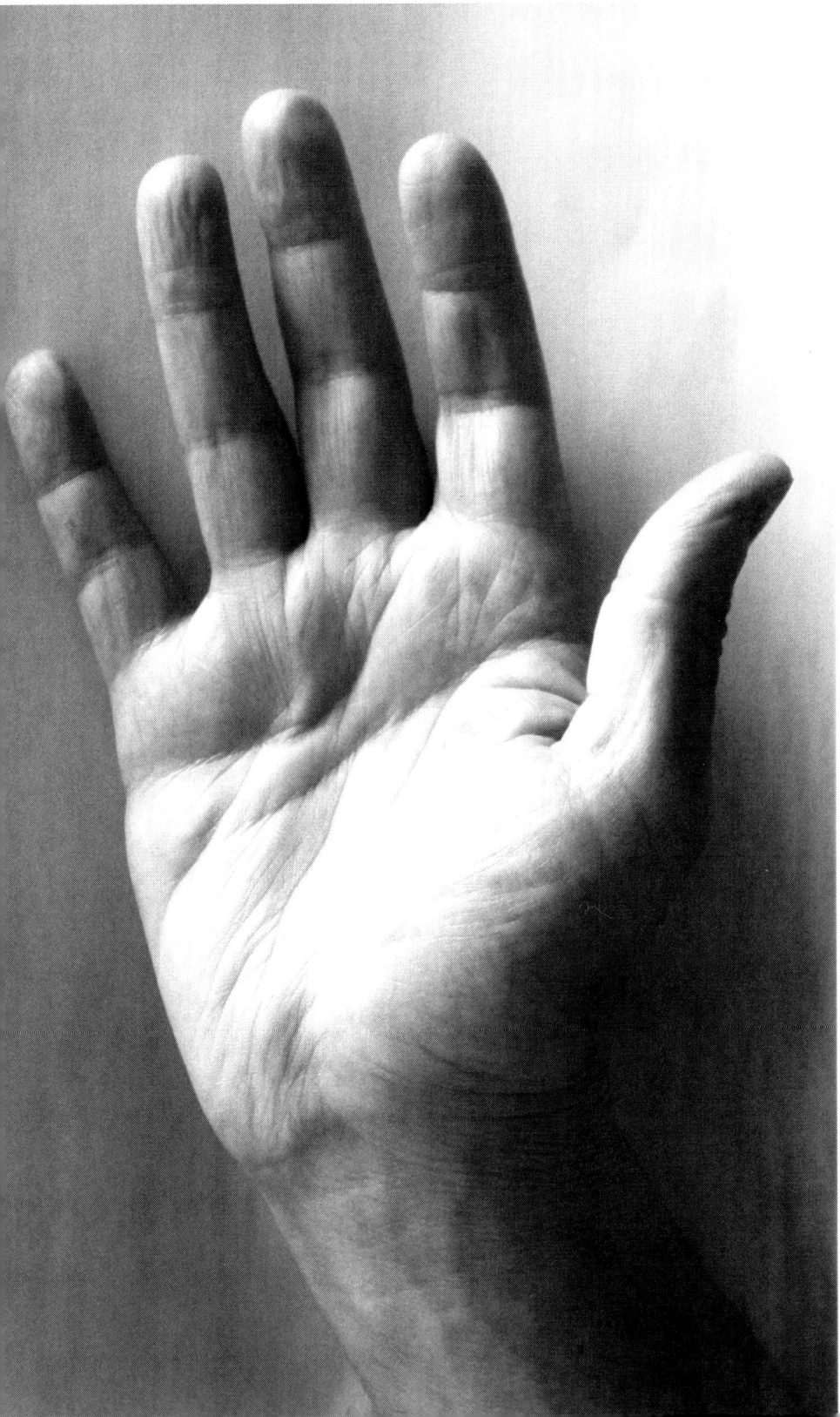

Lightning Source UK Ltd.
Milton Keynes UK
UKOW05f0333291213

223686UK00001B/21/P